There was a crooked man, and he went a
    crooked mile,
He found a crooked sixpence against a
    crooked stile;
He bought a crooked cat, which caught a
    crooked mouse,
And they all lived together in a little
    crooked house.

Anonymous
"There Was a Crooked Man"

IN PRAISE OF
*CATS*

SMITHMARK

*Producer:* Solomon M. Skolnick  *Designer:* Ann-Louise Lipman
*Editor:* Joan E. Ratajack  *Production:* Valerie Zars
*Photo Researcher:* Edward Douglas  *Assistant Photo
Researcher:* Robert V. Hale  *Editorial Assistant:*
Carol Raguso

Reprinted by permission of:

**Bertha Klausner International Literary Agency, Inc.:** Dorothy Baruch, "Cat," from *I Like Animals,*
copyright © 1963. **David Higham Associates Limited:** Eleanor Farjeon, "Cats," from *The Children's
Bells,* copyright © 1960, published by Oxford University Press. **Estate of Mary Britton Miller:** Mary
Britton Miller, "Cat," from *Menagerie,* copyright © 1928. **HarperCollins Publishers:** John Ciardi,
"Chang McTang McQuarter Cat," from *You Read to Me, I'll Read to You,* copyright © 1962 by John
Ciardi. **New Directions Publishing Corporation:** William Carlos Williams, "The Young Cat and the
Chrysanthemums," from *The Collected Poems of William Carlos Williams, 1939–1962, Vol. II,*
copyright © 1988. **The New Yorker Magazine, Inc.:** Rosalie Moore, "Catalogue," copyright © 1940,
1968. **Jean Pedrick:** Jean Pedrick, "Sleeping Cats." **Adam Yarmolinsky:** Babette Deutsch, "Black
Panther," from *The Collected Poems of Babette Deutsch,* copyright © 1969.

Index of Photographers

All photographs courtesy of The Image Bank. For information contact
The Image Bank, 111 Fifth Avenue, New York, N.Y. 10003

**Andy Caulfield** endpaper. **Barbara Kreye** 4. **Larry Dale Gordon** 5. **Ivor Sharp** 7. **Steve Proehl**
8, 15, 18. **Rob Atkins** 9. **Tim Bieber** 10-11. **Sebastiao Barbosa** 12. **Michael Melford** 13. **Lisl
Dennis** 14. **A.M. Rosario** 16. **Michael Skott** 17. **Brett Froomer** 19. **Cara Moore** 20, 21, 23, 27.
**Peter Miller** 24. **Larry Allen** 25. **Stephen Wilkes** 26. **Michael Quackenbush** 28-29.

Cats sleep fat and walk thin.
Cats, when they sleep, slump;
When they wake, stretch and begin
Over, pulling their ribs in.
Cats walk thin.

Rosalie Moore
"Catalogue"

The Cat. He walked
by himself, and all places
were alike to him.

Rudyard Kipling
*The Just-So Stories*
"The Cat That Walked By Himself"

One of the most striking differences
between a cat and a lie is that a cat
has only nine lives.

Mark Twain
*Pudd'nhead Wilson*
"Pudd'nhead Wilson's Calendar"

Chang McTang McQuarter Cat
Is one part this and one part that.
One part is yowl, one part is purr.
One part is scratch, one part is fur.
One part, maybe even two,
Is how he sits and stares right through
You and you and you and you.

John Ciardi
"Chang McTang McQuarter Cat"

Cruel, but composed and bland,
Dumb, inscrutable and grand,
So Tiberius might have sat,
Had Tiberius been a cat.

Matthew Arnold
"Poor Matthias"

Curiosity killed the cat, but satisfaction brought it back.

Popular saying

I put down my book
*The Meaning of Zen*
and see the cat smiling
    into her fur
as she delicately combs it
    with her rough pink tongue.

"Cat, I would lend you this
    book to study
but it appears that you have
    already read it."

She looks up and gives me
    her full gaze.
"Don't be ridiculous," she purrs.
    "I wrote it."

Dilys Laing
"Miao"

"All right," said the [Cheshire] Cat; and this time it vanished quite slowly, beginning with the end of the tail, and ending with the grin, which remained some time after the rest of it had gone.

Lewis Carroll
*Alice's Adventures in Wonderland*

From the sharp ears down to the finest hair
At his tail's tip, he might be carved of coal.
Child of the shadows, he appears as tame,
Till, from behind the grate, the gold eyes glare
With such a light as could consume the whole
To ashes and a memory of flame.

Babette Deutsch
"Black Panther"

Anywhere!
They don't care!
Cats sleep
Anywhere.

Eleanor Farjeon
"Cats"

Now my two old creatures
Sleep where the sun is streaming
And I wonder and wonder
And wonder what they're dreaming.

Jean Pedrick
"Sleeping Cats"

There wanst was two cats at Kilkenny,
Each thought there was one cat too many,
So they quarrell'd and fit,
They scratched and they bit,
Till, excepting their nails,
And the tips of their tails,
Instead of two cats, there warnt any.

Anonymous
"The Kilkenny Cats"

Watchcat is wild.
He runs the dark into a hole.
Keep your face away:
He doesn't play.

Mimi Drake
"Watchcat"

For I will consider my Cat Jeoffry,
For he is the servant of the Living God, duly
and daily serving him.

Christopher Smart
"My Cat Jeoffry"

All your wondrous wealth of hair,
Dark and fair,
Silken-shaggy, soft and bright
As the clouds and beams of night,
Pays my reverent hand's caress
Back with friendlier gentleness.

Algernon Charles Swinburne
"To a Cat"

Yes, you are lovely
with your ingratiating
manners, sleek sides and
small white paws. . . .

William Carlos Williams
"The Young Cat and the Chrysanthemums"

Louder he purrs and louder,
In one glad hymn of praise
For all the night's adventures,
For quiet, restful days.

Alexander Gray
''On a Cat Ageing''

Lifting herself
On her delicate toes,
She arches her back
As high as it goes.

Mary Britton Miller
"Cat"

Pure blood domestic, guaranteed,
Soft-mannered, musical in purr,
The ribbon had declared the breed,
Gentility was in the fur.

E.J. Pratt
"The Prize Cat"

My cat
Is quiet
She moves without a sound.
Sometimes she stretches herself curving
On tiptoe.
Sometimes she crouches low
And creeping.

Dorothy Baruch
"Cat"

Gaze
With those bright languid segments green, and prick
Those velvet ears—but prithee do not stick
Thy latent talons in me—and upraise
Thy gentle mew—and tell me all thy frays
Of fish and mice, and rats and tender chick.

John Keats
"To a Cat"

See the Kitten on the wall,
Sporting with the leaves that fall,
Withered leaves—one-two-and three—
From the lofty elder-tree!

William Wordsworth
"The Kitten and Falling Leaves"